Starting Your Dance Business

Anne Walker.

by

Anne Walker MBE

Grosvenor House
Publishing Limited

This book is published by
Grosvenor House Publishing Ltd
Link House
140 The Broadway, Tolworth, Surrey, KT6 7HT.
www.grosvenorhousepublishing.co.uk

A CIP record for this book
is available from the British Library

ISBN 978-1-78623-681-4

Foreword

I have known Anne Walker for probably about 40 years when she ran her own dance school in Crosby, Liverpool. As a young teacher I always looked up to her as she was an experienced and successful teacher, which is what I aspired to be. Anne has always been a helpful mentor to young teachers and currently to teachers of all ages (including myself) with her fabulous seminars that she runs across the country.

There is nothing more rewarding than having your own dance school. For many years I worked for full-time colleges, so the standard of student was usually exceptionally high. So when I opened my own school in 1993 I had to start from scratch with every single pupil in the school. Oh boy, was this hard work but so rewarding?

Many of the pupils I taught from day one are still involved in dance – teaching and performing. Others have moved on to other careers, but I am so proud of each and every one of them. I recently bumped into a past pupil onboard a cruise ship who I used to teach when she was only a child. She was performing as a professional act onboard and she was so excited to see me. Her words to me were, "You are taught by lots of teachers over the years, but some have a huge impact on you. You are one of those teachers who I am eternally grateful to for influencing my career and my life." These words make it all worthwhile.

If I had my time all over again, I would do exactly the same and open a dance school where my "Dance Family" are.

Good Luck to all young teachers embarking on their teaching careers.

Cathi Conroy-Jones.
   (Dance Teacher since 1980)

   Fellow and Triple International Examiner ISTD
   RAD Student Teaching Certificate
   Principal North Liverpool Dance Teacher Training College, ISTD Approved Centre
   Director UKDance Class Championships
   Ambassador Owen McVeigh Foundation

Acknowledgements

To everyone who bought my first book: thank you so much. You have given me the confidence to write this, my second book.

A massive thank you to my wonderful husband and my friends: I really could not do any of what I do without your love and support. A very special thank you to my wonderful mother who supported me every step of the way. She is, sadly, no longer with us, but, without her support, I would never have started my first school.

I am hugely grateful to Anthony Drewe for his permission to allow me to print his lyrics written for the stage musical of *Mary Poppins*. They continue to inspire me.

If you wish to learn more about starting, growing or running your dance business then you can discover more about Anne's Seminars at https://www.annewalker.com

Anne also offers mentoring and coaching via one-to-one meeting or video-call and you can follow her on Facebook at Anne Walker MBE.

Anne's first book *"Growing Your Dance Business"* is available from https://www.annewalker.com/

Contents

Introduction

So you want to own your own dance school. How very exciting! How incredibly daunting! This will be a life-changing decision if you decide this really is what you want to do for the next ten, twenty, thirty years or more. It will also be the most magical career when you consider how you will touch, and change for the better, the lives of so many young people and children. You will become a role model and mentor to many of your students and you will teach them so much more than just the dance styles they will learn at your studio. You will teach them self-respect, discipline, and team working. They will learn how to take correction, how to consider everyone in a group and not just worry about themselves, as well as learning that hard work and a disciplined approach to life really can make dreams come true.

Being the Principal of a dance school inevitably means you become a real part of your local community. You will be asked to take your students to perform at summer fetes or at local care homes. The local amateur dramatic groups may well ask you to choreograph or provide dancers for their shows and if you have a professional theatre in the vicinity, there may be opportunities for your students to perform there too.

This is all worth remembering when you decide to "take the plunge" and start your own dance business.

I started my first dance school aged only seventeen, having been inspired by seeing the *ballet "Sleeping Beauty"* at only eight years old. I certainly went on to learn the hard way. Having had two successful schools, I then founded and, for many years, ran International Dance Supplies which became a multi-million-pound global business. It was incredibly hard work, but fun too. I had to re-invent what we did, and how we did it, on many occasions, but this is what kept everyone focussed.

I want to share with you some of what I learned along the way, so you too, can have a profitable and successful business that gives you the lifestyle you deserve for all the hours and passion you put in to your enterprise.

Dream it, Do it, Make it Happen!

Chapter 1

Your Business Vision
First Thoughts

What made you realise you wanted to be a dance teacher? What made you realise you wanted your own school?

Perhaps you have been teaching for someone else and now you have decided it is time for you to have a business of your own. Or maybe you decided to train as a dance teacher as soon as you left school. Many professional dancers turn towards teaching once they decide to finish performing.

Where, when and how you start your own school will depend on many things:

- How much time are you able to devote to your new business? This will depend on if you already have a job or if this is to be your full-time occupation.

- Where will you hold your classes? This will depend on what facilities are available to hire (presumably you will not buy premises at the outset) in the area you plan to teach.
- Will you be a sole-trader or are you going into business with someone else and setting up a partnership or even a limited company?
- How will you recruit students into your school? How much marketing you are able to produce will depend on how much disposable cash you have. Perhaps you have been saving for years or maybe you need a loan or overdraft to get you started.

These are all vitally important decisions which should be made well in advance of your first classes. It is also essential that you are fully qualified to teach any subjects that you will personally teach. If you do not have any qualifications, then you would be well advised to set yourself up as the principal or director of the school and employ qualified teachers to actually teach your students. You can then continue your training until you have the required examination success. Many well-respected dance associations offer distance-learning qualifications which can be tailored to your specific needs. It is worth checking them out at https://cdmt.org.uk/validated-awarding-organisations

What sort of school are you planning to have? Will it be a multi-genre school or are you specialising in one specific type of dance or demographic? It is important to look to the future and not just consider the here-and-now. Although you might plan to just teach ballet to five-year-olds initially, consider a name for your business that reflects more than this very small range of classes. In the future, you may well employ tap and jazz teachers and remember that those five-year-olds will grow up, so consider all possibilities when you decide on a name for your business.

The name of your school must portray many things to many people. It needs to sound like a serious business, even though you may be planning fun classes for young children. The parents will want to be reassured that they are leaving their children in a safe, professional environment. If you will be including adult classes, then those students will also want to feel it is a school that is suitable for them. "Twinkly Toes" may not be giving quite the right image for your senior or adult classes as it does not sound like a commercial enterprise with a well-trained professional at the helm. However, it may be a perfect name for your pre-school ballet class.

Before making the final decision on your business name, make thorough checks that the domain name is available for your website and check that no one else anywhere near you has the same, or similar-sounding name.

Now is also a good time to check that you will not be holding your classes very close to an existing school and you should never seek to hire a venue in the same building as someone else.

If you are already a member of a teaching organisation or society, you will be signed up to their code of professional conduct as part of your membership. This will include a section covering not stepping on the toes of other teachers. For example; "A teacher should behave with integrity in all professional and business relationships. Integrity implies not merely honesty but fair dealing, courtesy and consideration" This statement has many considerations including that you really should not rent the same hall or premises that another teacher is already hiring. Even though they may not teach on the day that you wish to use the room, it is still very unprofessional to seek to hire the same premises or even somewhere in the same road as another teacher. Consider how you would feel if someone did that to you!

If you are unsure about the details of your Professional Code of Conduct you should first check with your association or awarding body. For teachers in the UK, the Council for Dance, Drama and Musical Theatre (CDMT) does have a good example on this page of their website (scroll down the page) https://cdmt.org.uk/part-time-learning/apply-now

What will make your school stand out from your competitors? What do you offer that is different from other schools? It is only a few lucky schools who do not have direct competition. Do you have a USP? This is your Unique Selling Proposition. It is what makes your school standout and what makes your business different to your competitors. If you are setting up your new studio in an area that is crowded with dance schools, then you need to promote your USP as much as possible.

Almost as important as these practicalities is the VISION you have for your future and that of your business. Your passion for dance has probably made you choose this career path, but you need to have some goals and objectives to help you on that journey from these small beginnings to achieve the business you want to own.

Buy a notepad and write down your vision and dreams for yourself and your business. You could include your long-term goals as well as your mission statement, remembering the ethos behind why you are doing this and the overall reasons for starting your business.

Once you have written this, consider your short-term goals. What will you have to do at every step along the way in order to achieve your vision? These will change over the years as you achieve some of your goals, but you must have an initial plan.

I am a huge believer in the statement that, "You can't grow bigger than your dreams," so start with some pretty large ambitions and you can always "tweak" them as the business progresses.

Make It Happen!

1   What is your dream? Write it down now
2   Write down your 1-year/2-year/5-year goals
3   Believe you can make them happen
4   Start to share these goals with people around you
5   Remember: You can't grow bigger than your dreams, so dream as big as you dare!

Chapter 2

Right from the start

It really is vitally important that you think of and run your school as a business and a professional enterprise **Right from the start.**

You will need the students and their parents to trust you and to respect you as a business person, no matter if you have five or 50 pupils. If you start as though it is just a hobby or in an amateurish way, it will be very difficult to become more business-like as you grow.

You have possibly not been to business school so the main inspiration behind your dance school could well be the dance teacher who instilled a love of dance in you when you were very young. Those memories will be very precious and important to you, but **time has moved on.** There are now so many more rules, regulations and procedures with which you must comply, that it is essential you consider them from the very concept of your school. You need to think like a business person and a professional from the very beginning. Your school should be run as a commercial enterprise from the moment you create it. A business needs to make money in order to grow and develop. If you do not make a profit you will be unable to develop yourself or pay for your on-going professional training (CPD – continuing professional development), you will be unable to take on any extra teachers or other staff and your business will not be able to grow or thrive.

Even if you want to support any students who are unable to pay the full fees you must firstly run your school successfully. Once you are running it profitably, then you will have the resources to be able to offer support to others.

Perhaps one of the most important considerations is what you will call your new business. As with many things in business this can be a crucial decision and you may be surprised as to what a difference the correct name will make to how you are viewed by your students, prospective students and their parents. You must include your name and the business name on all official documents such as invoices and letters.

Now is the time to start your Business Plan. There area many free examples available online, or your business bank might offer a template you could follow. If your business is in the UK there is help available as well as templates here: https://www.gov.uk/browse/business/setting-up You will also find information about start-up loans here. Or, if you are aged under 30, you may be able to receive help and support to set up your business from the Prince's Trust www.princes-trust.org.uk/

This is also a good time to consider your long-term goals. You may start out teaching just one genre of dance, but if your ambition is to have a school covering many different aspects of dance then a title that states this would be a sensible option now. Likewise, if you are planning to cover dance, drama and musical theatre, then now is the right time to have a name that is all-encompassing.

If you are starting your business in a local church or village school, be wary of using the name of the town in your title. What will happen if you need to move to a venue in another locality? Once you have established your school name with all the additional named business items (website, bank account, credit card, social media, etc.) it can be a real pain to change the name, so it is in your best interests to choose a suitable title from the very beginning.

Once you have established your business name and format (i.e. Sole-trader, partnership, limited company) the next thing to do is to buy your website domain name to ensure none of your competitors buy it! This may seem far-fetched but, believe me, it happens, and it did actually happen to me once! If you can afford it, buy all the domains that relate to your school name. You will only require one website, but, if correctly set up, all the other web addresses will take anyone searching on those words, to your site.

Now you have your web address, you will also have the ability to use emails which relate to it. I beg of you to use this as soon as you own it rather than a free email address. Which looks more professional?

- Annedancingfeetwalker1978@hotmail.com
- anne@walkerschoolofdance.com

I hope you can easily see which looks more professional. It is a fact that your customers are nine times more likely to trust you if you use a professional email address.

Most people would never consider using a lawyer, surgeon, architect or any other professional who had a silly email address, so you should not expect your clients to use one for you. Besides which, by always using your school domain name for your emails it is free, subliminal advertising. Why advertise Hotmail or other businesses when you can be advertising your own business every time you send or receive an email? It inspires trust in your business and makes everyone aware, when you are using it, that this is an important, business email, which they should be taking seriously. This will help you in so many ways as your business develops.

A Business Plan is always a sensible way to begin a new enterprise. If you are borrowing any money from a bank you will be required to produce a business plan before they agree to your loan, but you would be well advised to write one however you are managing your funding.

There are many free templates available online, including (for businesses in UK) this one https://www.princes-trust.org.uk/help-for-young-people/tools-resources/business-tools/business-plans and https://www.gov.uk/government/publications/starting-and-growing-a-home-business-advice-and-support also has huge amounts of help if you are just setting up a business in the UK. Search the internet for examples and business plan templates in your country.

Both these websites also offer advice on funding for start-up businesses and many geographical areas will have local enterprise or business partnerships who may be able to help with funding or grants. It is pretty time consuming to search through all the potential funding sources but definitely worth the time spent and you will probably learn other useful information at the same time.

Remember, this may be a new business, but it is YOURS, so do not let parents or your competitors persuade you to do something in a way that is not what you feel is right. Do not become embroiled in gossiping about other schools and do not post anything detrimental about others on your social media pages. Keep everything professional right from the start of your business.

Make It Happen!

1 Do everything **Right** from the start
2 Choose your Business Name
3 Buy your domain names relating to your business
4 Immediately start using your email address relating to your domain name
5 Write your Business Plan

Chapter 3

Your Brand
Who you are and what you stand for

As soon as you have decided on the fundamentals of your new business you need to consider your brand.

- What will it stand for?
- What makes it unique to you?
- What impact will it have on your customers and potential customers?

What do you think of when someone mentions brand or branding? The logo is probably what most people immediately recall, and maybe also a colour or tagline. Branding is so much more than that and, if you get it right, can have a massively positive impact on your business.

Branding is incredibly powerful and should run through everything you do and every aspect of your business.

The dictionary definition is possibly not what you imagine:

The process involved in creating a unique name and image for a product in the consumers mind. Branding aims to establish a significant and differentiated presence in the market that attracts and retains loyal customers.

This is exactly what you need to be doing. You should make sure that everyone can easily tell what is different about your school as soon as they see your website, your flyers, social media and all your marketing.

It is absolutely essential that you are very clear in your own mind, about all aspects of your brand, long before you start to advertise your new business. The way you use your branding will determine how people in your local community, as well as in the dance industry, will see your business. They should be able to tell that you are serious about this new business and that you are a responsible and professional business owner. This is important at whatever age you start a business, but it is absolutely essential if you are a young teacher straight out of college. You need your clients and students, as well as everyone in the local community, to treat you seriously and to respect you and your wishes. This will become apparent as soon as you are asking for money for fees/costumes/rehearsals/etc. Everyone must know who is in charge!

Think about the logo that suits your business name. Keep it as simple as possible and make sure it is appropriate for your planned clientele. Also think about the future. A logo that is pink and pretty, with a little ballerina, may be fine for now but will not work so well if you are launching a street dance class or a boy's ballet class.

Do not use an image that others can use. Your logo should be unique to you. Either have someone design it for you (make sure they hand over the copyright to you) or use an image that you have photographed or drawn yourself.

What colour(s) will you choose? The colour of your logo, lettering and branding, can often, unwittingly, send out the wrong message. Red and yellow usually represents "Sale" or "discount" (think of sale banners in shop windows) and red can also be seen as threatening. This is a colour that should be used sparingly in your logo or marketing.

Green is seen as restful, natural and can indicate prosperity, especially if mixed with gold, although many theatrical people may be superstitious about green and consider it brings bad luck. Brown can look rather old-fashioned, but blues are generally seen as indicating trust, reliability and calmness. ?

For many people, pink used to be the colour of ballet but there are many shades of pink as well as purple that can be used to indicate vibrancy and positivity. Black and white will always be the clearest to read and the cheapest to reproduce, and, where possible, use black print on a white background as the reverse is difficult to read. In fact, many people are simply unable to read white text even if it is on a dark background. Naturally, in some parts of the world colours may take on different meanings. Even once you have chosen the colour or colours to represent your brand, there are still many different shades from which you can choose.

Next you must consider typeface. Choose a simple, clear, easy-to-read typeface for your business name so that it can be read quickly and easily wherever you use it. It should be just as easy for someone to read your logo and business name in a small advert in a local newspaper as it is to read it across the street on a large banner. The same applies to all written communication. Using a script typeface does not fool people into thinking you have hand-written the message – it just prevents them from easily reading it and so they could very well miss completely the important message you are trying to portray.

You could consider a "strap line" or "tag line" as part of your branding too. One of the great positives of using a strapline is that it can easily be changed if you alter any aspects of your business. However, it is important to ensure your school name and the strap line always complement each other and explain what the business actually does. For example; if your business is called xxx School of Dance and Performing Arts, your tagline could be "Performing is our Passion". However, if the business is called xxx Academy you need to make your tagline describe what the academy teaches, so it could perhaps be "Where dance, drama and singing are brought to life". These are not particularly great examples, but I hope you understand the point!

As I mentioned earlier, if you should change disciplines or add more genres to your school, your tagline can easily be altered to make changes. It is so much more difficult to change a name, but the tagline can grow as your business develops.

Make It Happen!

1. Choose a colour for your brand
2. Choose a typeface for your brand
3. What is your logo?
4. What is your strapline?
5. Check everything looks cohesive and part of the same business

Chapter 4

Marketing and Communication

In the early days of your business, marketing will be vital. In fact, you would be well advised to start marketing your business several months ahead of your launch date. Building anticipation, and a sense of excitement, will help your first few days of teaching feel like a bigger event than it may actually be. If you are worried about your potential competitors finding out about your plans, then you may need to be a little cautious, but, if you are following your professional code of conduct (see addendum A) you really have nothing to worry about. Competition from other dance schools will help to keep you focussed about what makes your school different (and, hopefully, better) than your competitors.

The most successful form of marketing will be by word of mouth and personal recommendation. Talk about your plans to everyone you know and anyone you meet. The more people that know about your school and when you are launching it, the better. Encourage your friends to tell their friends and the word will soon spread.

You should approach your local radio stations too and see if they are willing to interview you. This may sound terrifying, but the presenters are generally very skilled at interviewing and all you have to do is share your passion. Try and make it really sound like a local interest story, rather than blatant advertising and be careful to talk about what your school will offer that is different from others.

Find out the name of the shows host who interviews either local business owners or regularly has a young peoples feature. Email them with your exciting plans and remember to follow it up if they do not respond to your message.

You should try the same route with your local newspapers. Yes! People do still read newspapers. And even regional or local magazines. Remember it may be a grandparent of a potential student who reads the piece rather than a parent.

Setting up all these contacts ahead of your business launch will be really useful as your school expands. Keep a list of all editors/broadcasters with whom you have worked in the past and make sure you tell them

EVERYTHING that happens in your school as it grows. This is all PR and is absolutely invaluable as well as being completely FREE!

So far, this has all been free marketing. What else can you do that costs nothing?

Social media is another great way to start building your business. At this point in your business you are building awareness of your brand as well as your classes. Make it as easy as possible for people to ask for more information as well as encouraging them to "like" your page.

Whatever you do, keep your personal social media pages completely separate from your business pages and do not be tempted to let parents or prospective students become personal "friends". Stay professional at all times and keep your business posts businesslike.

Google places is also free, so set that up as soon as possible. Be careful not to use your home address for the venue, or you might well have a picture of your house appearing here! Not very professional!

Give yourself plenty of time to set up all your social media, Google places, etc. Think about the future as well as the here and now. Consider photographs and how they should be used. Who owns the copyright? It is possible to buy, fairly reasonably, stock images that are copyright free and ideal for starting your marketing campaign. Never use pictures of your own students without being certain their parent or guardian has signed your consent form, even if it is a casual shot taken on your phone in class.

Plan your marketing campaign. Include everything. Decide in advance what you want it to deliver. Be specific about your targets. For example;

FB posts	twice weekly	raise awareness
Local press	monthly	sign-up 10 new students
Local radio	once launch day	raise awareness

You will need to word your adverts or posts differently depending on what you want to achieve and who your target audience is.

You may consider having some flyers printed. There are many things to think about now! Here are some thoughts:

1. Print on both sides of the paper (the main cost is the paper so don't waste the second side)

2. Your business name and logo plus tagline, if you have one, must be in the top section of the page
3. Telephone number, website, email or other contact information should be on BOTH sides (make it as easy as possible for the person reading it)
4. Try and sound as though you are talking to just one person. Do not use phrases like "you may all be interested" Make it a definite "your child will love this class"
5. You need a call to action "Book your place today"
6. Use a simple typeface and black ink on a lighter background
7. Remember to incorporate your school colours and branding
8. It is fine to use a free design app (like Canva) but double check everything and then get someone else to check the grammar and spelling too
9. Keep it as simple as possible while still giving out all the relevant information
10. WIFM (what's in it for me) That is ALL the person reading it wants to know, so make sure that is obvious (Enrol before xxx for your discounted fee)

Do you know what your USP will be? This stands for Unique Selling Proposition. It is what makes you different from all the other dance schools. Be sure you know what it is and how it fits in with your brand. You might be the only teacher in the area teaching contemporary. You might run specialist boys' classes or be the only school in the area that teaches Flamenco. That is your USP. Be sure that everyone knows what it is. Make it part of your branding so prospective students and their parents realise why they MUST sign up to your school rather than your competitors.

Verbal communication with your students and their parents or guardians is something that you need to think about. Flippantly saying things at the end of a class, when you are rushing to start the next class, can frequently lead to misunderstanding on all sides. Important messages should always be given to everyone at the same time, so email has to be the most effective. Use a system like https://mailchimp.com/ and then you can check if and when the message was opened and you can rest assured that it is General Data Protection Regulation (GDPR) compliant. Always repeat really important messages, but make sure you say the same thing again. Mixed messages just confuse everyone.

Remember most parents who bring their children to your classes will lead busy lives, possibly with siblings going to other activities as well as your classes. They will not necessarily treat messages from you with the importance or urgency you require. It is up to you to ensure they realise your messages really are important. Do not get into the habit of blaming the parent for everything. Maybe you need to make your messages clearer or easier to understand the key points.

Make It Happen!

1. Plan your marketing strategy
2. Tell everyone you know that you are starting a business
3. Build your social media business profile
4. Start making contacts in the media
5. Keep your brand and USP visible at all times

Chapter 5

Support

Starting your own school was probably your idea so it will very much feel like your own "baby" and you will feel very precious about how you want to run and develop it. You will, almost inevitably, want to control everything!

Believe me, will need all the help you can get if you want to grow your school into a successful and profitable business. This is one thing I really wish I had known when I was just starting out in business. The more you network with other successful business owners (in any occupation) the more you will learn about how to do things correctly and successfully in your own business. And the more inspired you are likely to be too.

As well as support from other businesspeople you will meet, you should receive help and support from your accountant. In the very early days, you may wonder if an accountant is really necessary. However, they may well become your greatest support as your business grows. It is worth finding someone who has helped other businesses to grow as they will be able to support you through many of the challenges you will face. They will also be able to look at your business in an unemotional way – unlike you! – and challenge you to think differently.

Support may well come from a family member, but make sure they realise that this is a business you are setting up and not just a hobby. An involved family member must understand your brand and your ethos. They may well get roped in to answer the phone or to respond to messages, so be sure to explain to them how you want this done. It is an important part of your brand and your professionalism.

There are now a number of mentors in the dance industry. I have been mentoring dance teachers and other small business owners for the last twenty years and I know how useful it can be. When you are feeling as though you have all the problems of the world on your shoulders it is very useful to have someone you know you can turn to either on an occasional basis or a regular session. With technology now, you can have a "face to face" conversation even though you are many miles, or even countries, apart.

You can seek the support of the examination body to which you belong. Many of them have someone at head office who will be able to answer your questions and they probably have self-help groups on social media too. Although you should try not to be pulled in, to the negativity that emanates from some of these groups! In the UK the CDMT (The council for dance, drama and musical theatre provides quality assurance for the professional dance, drama and musical theatre industries) offers help and support for teachers via their website https://cdmt.org.uk/ as well as countrywide conferences. Other countries will have similar awarding bodies and support groups. It is worth taking the time to investigate how much support is available for free.

As I mentioned earlier, the more you mix and network with other successful business owners the more inspired you will be. It is difficult when you are starting a business to make time to go to meetings and events, but you will reap the rewards over time. It might even be worthwhile considering joining the Federation of Small Businesses (FSB) https://www.fsb.org.uk/ This not-for-profit organisation cover the whole of the UK and aims to help smaller businesses achieve their ambitions. There is an annual membership fee, but they offer so much free help and support that you could save your membership fee in the first couple of months.

For example, there is a Health and Safety helpline which you can call for free advice as well as policy documents and guidance which you can freely download, as well as free Health and Safety factsheets.

Free legal advice and business banking are just two other areas that can save you huge amounts of money as well as the ease of finding all this support in one place.

Your government website will offer help when setting up a business. In the UK you should look at https://www.gov.uk/set-up-business but other countries will have similar information available. This helps you through the various forms of a business and whether you will be classed as employed or self-employed and is a really useful tool for your business now and in the future.

Don't be alone. There is lots of help and support out there. You will be glad you used it, but you will have to make time to do your research. Making time to network now will mean you have a ready-made network of support as and when your business expands. So many successful business owners will be only too happy to pass on their knowledge and experience to someone just starting their business, so do not be afraid to ask.

Make It Happen!

1. Talk to other successful business owners
2. Your accountant should be a supporter of and for your business
3. Ensure family members know this is a business
4. Find a mentor who inspires you
5. Join a support group like https://www.fsb.org.uk/

Chapter 6

Policies, Procedures and Contracts

You may think you do not need to worry about any of these until your business is established and you are employing people. WRONG!

Remember, Chapter 2 was called "Right From the Start", well, here are some of the things you need to get right, right from the start of your business. It may seem a bit of a waste of time but do it now and then all you have to do is simply renew and review everything every year.

You will need at least the following (and in some countries you may well need other licences or permits too):

1. Insurance. (public liability and professional indemnity
2. DBS (disclosure and baring service) check
3. Children and vulnerable adult protection policy
4. Health & Safety policy

5. PPL PRS Music licence
6. Privacy/GDPR policy
7. Equal opportunities policy
8. Customer service policy
9. A contract with any premises that you hire
10. If you are running your business from home, you may need planning permission as well as permission from your mortgage lender

Procedures are a planned way of achieving an outcome. You should have a procedure for many of the items on the above list for example: You have a Health & Safety Policy, but you must have a PROCEDURE that you can work through to ensure your Health & Safety Policy complies with the law.

Let us look at the above list in more detail.

INSURANCE

- Public liability insurance is essential. It covers you in case anyone you are teaching suffers a personal injury or even death. Without insurance, if the worst should happen and you are sued by the parent or a family member it could completely ruin you and your career.
- Professional Indemnity Insurance is also a safeguard and may well be a requirement of any venue you hire.

- Don't forget car insurance too. You need to be very clear as to how you are using your vehicle for work. Do you leave expensive equipment, laptop, etc overnight? Are you ever likely to take a student to an exam or performance as a passenger in your car?

Your insurer will need to know the sort of classes you teach, and you will be charged according to the risks posed by your classes. You may find it helpful to check if your membership body recommends an insurance company or you could use an insurance broker. They will check different companies to find the most cost-effective solution for your requirements.

Remember to inform your insurance company or broker if your classes increase or you add new classes. Failure to do so could make any insurance policies you hold, null and void.

DBS

- You, and anyone else involved in your business who has any contact with your students, will require a DBS (disclosure and baring service) or similar check, depending in which country your school is located. This will become a requirement for your children and vulnerable adult protection policy.

Children and vulnerable adult protection policy

You will be able to obtain a free template, that you can brand with your school name, from the NSPCC or the equivalent in your country. https://learning.nspcc.org.uk/safeguarding-child-protection/

There you will also find other useful information as well as on-line or face-to-face training opportunities which will generally count towards your CPD (continuing professional development).

Health & Safety policy

Again, there are free templates to download available online as well as at https://cdmt.org.uk/ Remember to add your own branding to any template and keep it short and simple. You may need a specific page for each venue you hire if they are very different. For example, a church or village hall will need a more simple form than a theatre or multi-purpose venue. Your Health & Safety policy may well be mandatory for the venues you hire as well as your insurance. Venues may also insist that you show a PAT test certificate for all the electrical items you use (speakers, adaptors, cables, etc) and risk assessments should always be readily available for all the premises you use.

Music licences

You must pay a fee to play any sort of music unless you own the copyright yourself. This is to ensure that the composer, songwriter and publisher all receive due compensation for their work. In the UK this is all collected and distributed by the recent merging of two companies (PPL and PRS) and is now known as The Music Licence. All details and how to work out your costs is available here: https://pplprs.co.uk/themusiclicence/ Other countries have similar schemes. Check your government website for more information.

This is most definitely a cost of running your business that you need to remember and record. Your licence fee will be paid annually and will increase as your school expands.

Privacy/GDPR policy

Because you hold information about your students either electronically or on a manual system you are bound by law to register with the Information Commissioner's Office. In the UK this can be done via their website https://ico.org.uk/

No matter how much, or how little, information you hold you must sign up and pay a small annual fee.

Name, address, date of birth all counts as data and there are rules about how you are allowed to keep and use this information. In the UK, not following these rules can incur a fine and will certainly not be sending out the right message about your business. Many other countries have similar data-protection laws.

Always remember: Ignorance of the law excuses no one. Get some online training now and make your business robust and professional. Your training will also add to your CPD (continuing professional development) portfolio.

Equal opportunities policy

More than ever before, it is now vital to have an equal opportunities policy.

Your business must offer equal opportunities to everyone including your students, parents, any staff you may employ as well as the general public. A simple template is available from https://cdmt.org.uk/ and more information is available from your government website.

Customer service policy

You may think, as a dance school, you do not require a customer service policy, but you are delivering customer service the same as any other business and you may as well consider all aspects of running a great business right from the start.

Devise a simple customer service policy that is easy to manage but it will help you to ensure you are always striving to deliver a professional and efficient service to all customers whether they are parents, guardians, students or other teachers.

As before, there is a great template here for you to personalise with your own brand and ethos: https:// cdmt.org.uk/ or you may find your teaching association has one that you can share.

Contracts

Contracts are essential for the safe and effective running of your business. You will require many different ones throughout the life of your school, so the sooner you get used to automatically thinking about them the better!

You will need a contract with your students or their parents. This will state what they can expect from you (e.g. 10 classes per term, extra coaching or show rehearsals) and what you can expect from them (e.g. terms fees to be paid in full by the third week of term or their child will be excluded. How much notice they must give you if they wish to withdraw their child). This should be a very simple "contract" which they must sign, as soon as they enrol their child, to say they accept all your terms and conditions. This will help to stop any unpleasantness later. This should be part of the enrolment process and may be tied in with a registration or joining fee. It will save time in the future too if parents give their permission here for such things as being in photographs which may be used on your website or social media.

It is essential you have a contract with any venues that you hire. Ensure there is a clause that stops another dance teacher using the same premises for their classes. This may not seem important to you when you start your school but, if the venue is let to another dance teacher – possibly even someone teaching a genre that you do not teach – there is nothing to stop them starting classes similar to yours in the future. This could be very detrimental to your business. It is totally unprofessional, but sadly, that does not always stop your competitors. Make sure you always adhere to a professional code of conduct and hopefully you will encourage other local teachers to do so too.

You will certainly need a contract of employment if you employ anyone else at all in the school or a contract for freelance or self-employed staff. This must include any office help you may take on as well as teachers and class assistants.

Once again, there are some great templates here: https://cdmt.org.uk/ Once you start to think about shows or performances then more contracts will be required; with the theatre as well as for hire of lighting and effects etc.

If the other party offers you a contract, always make sure you are happy with the terms and conditions and negotiate with them if changes need making. If none is offered, then proffer your own. In the case of staff UK law dictates that you must offer them a contract. If in doubt, check with a qualified lawyer.

Make It Happen!

1. Buy your insurance policies
2. Obtain your DBS or equivalent check
3. Write up all your policies
4. Pay your music and data protection fees
5. Check any permissions which may be required and remember:
    Ignorance of the law excuses no one

Chapter 7

Financials

A sound understanding of the financial aspects of your business will give you a stable basis that will enable you to grow a successful and profitable enterprise. It will be so much easier to have knowledge of some basic principles of financial management now while your school is relatively small. Hopefully, your expertise will grow as your business does.

Find a bank that is able to support your business. Do they offer a business account? It is certainly worth looking around and comparing what they offer.

Assuming you are not a trained accountant, it really will pay you to build a strong working connection with a local account. Ask around other small businesses (not just dance schools) and find the names of some local accountants that you could meet. Preferably someone who has helped and supported other businesses as they have grown. You need someone that you can trust completely and that you feel comfortable asking for help.

However, it is also important that you take the financials seriously. Ask your accountant how best to keep your records so that it will be simple for you and easy for them. This will make the whole process easier and definitely cheaper. A good accountant will not actually cost you anything, as their fee should more than cover whatever they save you in taxes or other costs.

One of the key challenges is to make sure you allow time to commit to your bookkeeping. Schedule some time in, every week, no matter how busy you are. This will become a very good habit that will make life so much easier as your business grows. It also means you will be able to understand just where you stand financially at any given time. This is particularly useful if something unexpected happens (e.g. class numbers increase, and you need to take on an assistant or you suddenly need to rent a more expensive venue).

You will certainly need to accept payment via credit/ debit card, so do make sure you have shopped around for the most cost-effective solution. You need to take in to account the percentage you will be charged for the use of this facility and it can vary enormously between the different providers. Regular monthly payments will certainly help your customers to stay on top of the fees. You should consider a registration fee. Although not all dance schools charge one, most other groups charge some sort of enrolment or joining fee and it is another way to keep your fees reasonable as you are gaining extra income from this one-off fee. You can make it an annual fee if you wish. However, it then becomes a "membership" fee and you may find there are certain laws which apply so check this out thoroughly.

Do not be tempted to set your fees lower than everyone else in your area. You have trained long and hard for your qualifications and you should never under-sell yourself. Keep your prices fair and increase them a small amount every year. If you do not, and then you suddenly have to increase them massively, you will upset more people than if you gradually increase them regularly once a year.

You may well find it difficult to discuss fees and other payments. Automate as much as possible and do not be persuaded to charge less than you believe you are worth. If anyone is late paying, deal with it as soon as possible. The longer you leave it, the harder you will find it is to chase them. This is when membership of an organisation like the Federation of Small Businesses (FSB) https://www.fsb.org.uk/ is so valuable as they will help you chase outstanding debts.

Make It Happen!

1. Find a bank who will support your business
2. Find a great accountant and get to know them
3. Schedule time to manage your finances
4. Organise a credit card system and/or direct debit
5. Set your fees

Chapter 8

Your First Show

This will probably be one of the most stressful parts of running your business but also one of the most rewarding. Every time you start your plans for a show or performance, you will swear it will be the LAST TIME, but then, on show night, you realise you LOVE it and of course so do the students, parents and everyone else who travel miles to see your production.

Before you can start the preparations, you need to find a suitable venue. If you have lots of young children who will be performing, it is important to have an easily accessible theatre, with good car parking facilities, even a school hall might work when your school is just in its infancy. The next challenge is where all those children can safely and securely get changed and wait between numbers or performances.

The show and rehearsal dates will always cause controversy so choose what works for you and your business, and then give everyone involved as much notice as possible.

The next legal challenge is the licences most local authorities (in UK and elsewhere) will require you to obtain for your students aged below the school leaving age. They will also require supervision by licenced chaperones. This will vary greatly from area to area, even in the UK, so check out as many of these regulations as possible months in advance of your performance. You will also be required to have all your policies up to date as well as insurance which covers the performance. I really cannot stress enough how this must be planned well in advance.

How will you fund your show? There will be many costs including:

Venue hire for show and rehearsals
Chaperone licences
Costumes
Costume rails/hangers
Accessories/props
Scenery/backcloths
Lighting/extension cables
Printing of tickets/flyers/programmes
Music editing
Photographer/videographer
Thank-you gifts and cards

Some schools will fundraise during the year so costumes can be kept by the school for use in future events. Other schools will buy in the costumes and accessories and either sell them on to the students or hire them out for a fee. It is entirely your choice and very much depends on a) if you can afford to buy lots of costumes and b) you have space to keep them all. It might be worth selling some on but keeping some basic accessories (bowler hats for example) as well as sets of good basic costumes which could be styled differently in the future.

Choose costumes carefully. You will have all shapes and sizes of children in your classes. Make sure the outfit is suitable for all of them as well as being age appropriate. Choose music that is age appropriate too. It is unsuitable for youngsters to be performing to suggestive lyrics even if they do know all the words. Remember children grow! If you buy your costumes months ahead of performance, make sure you have allowed some space for growth spurts or at least an extra outfit or two.

Music should be professionally edited unless you are extremely good and always have a plan B at the theatre. You never know what may happen!

Props can be extremely useful, as it gives the students something to do with their hands and arms, so you only have to worry about their feet! However, a word of warning, props can be dropped!

The more disciplined you are in class with your students, the easier it will be to control them all backstage. If you have been a performer yourself, you will understand how important it is to rehearse the stage entrances and exits. If you have not experienced this my advice would be to rehearse it as much as possible, especially if any of it will take place in a black-out. That can be pretty scary for your little children.

If you are not an experienced performer, take some time to learn some of the technical terms used in a theatre. The technical crew will expect you to know what they are talking about and will expect a professional approach from you and there is a great book **#AYN2K Dance Studio Edition** which is available from http://wwaudio.co.uk/

Think very carefully about your running order. If performers are in multiple numbers, quick changes will need to be managed very carefully and safely, so the fewer of these you schedule, the better.

You need to consider every last little detail about the time spent in your performance venue. Will the performers be allowed to eat or drink in their costumes? Will they come with hair and make-up done or will you need to allocate a room and people to do it at the venue?

Who will be your First Aid Provider? Charities like St John Ambulance will often provide support, for a donation.

Your Health & Safety policy and risk assessments will need to reflect the venue and facilities as well as taking into account any extra equipment you have hired.

The selling of tickets can waste a huge amount of your time, so I would definitely recommend using a third party like Stage Stubbs http://stagestubs.com/ or similar. You will have none of the hassle but should receive your money in a timely fashion.

You will need all your lists, policies and licences available at the performances just in case you have an inspection from your local authority.

Finally, try and enjoy the process and the event. Your students will gain so much from performing and it is a fantastic showcase for your school. It is a great way to bring more students into your school (as they will come and see their friends and hopefully then want to join themselves!) as well as inspiring your current students to take an extra class or to just stick at it so they can be like the older students.

Make It Happen!

1. Book your venue
2. Share your show dates with everyone
3. Check out licensing requirements
4. Make a schedule with EVERYTHING on it
5. Rehearse at the venue as much as possible

Chapter 9

Your First Exam Session

Unless you have chosen never to enter your students for exams or medal tests, you will eventually have to face your first exam session. Exams are a great way to give your students a sense of achievement and often parents are keen for their children to take part in exams as they will receive a certificate or medal which can be on display at home or shared with granny and grandma!

Remember there are many different examining bodies as well as the one with which you gained your qualifications, so it is worth looking at all the options to find the format that best suits your school.

Exam day can be a very exciting time for your students, and they should be excited to show off what they have learned, to the examiner. This will also be the first time a professional "outsider" will have been into your business so you must plan ahead to ensure the examiner has a wonderful day and a really positive experience whilst they are in your studio.

If your examiner is happy, warm and well looked after, they will be more relaxed and therefore more able to enjoy the day. If the students see the examiner looking happy, they can relax too and hopefully perform their best work.

Well in advance of your session you should consider the space available. Where will the examiner sit? They will need a table that is large enough for their paperwork, a bell (which you must provide), a jug/bottle of water and a glass (also provided by you). A tablecloth always looks like you have made an effort and a few flowers in a small vase are a welcome touch but make sure the examiner still has a clear view of the room and all the candidates. The chair should be a suitable height, and a cushion and a rug on a nearby chair are generally welcome. Make sure you have sat in the chair for hours at a time (maybe at your exam rehearsal) to make sure it is comfy for a long examining day. It really is in your best interests (and the best interests of the candidates) to ensure the examiner feels warm and well looked after.

It is always worth remembering that the examiner may have travelled a long way to get to your studio so make sure they know exactly where they can park (if they are driving) and warn them in advance if they will have to pay for parking. A reserved space near the studio entrance is always a good idea and ensure your school name is visible somewhere on the outside of the building so everyone knows they are in the correct venue.

If they are coming by public transport, it is always a good idea to arrange to collect them from the station or airport.

When you first meet your examiner, greet them as Miss/ Mrs/Mr (not by their Christian name) and introduce yourself. Once in the studio introduce the person who is playing your music and make sure they have a comfortable chair too and are not visible by the candidates.

The examiner may like a tea or coffee after their journey, and you should also point out where the toilet is that they can use. Clean soap and towels are essential. If there is a toilet that the students are not using so much the better, although this is not always possible. However, the students should not be changing inside the studio, even if the area is cordoned off.

Before the first candidates enter the room, tell the examiner of any last-minute changes or anything else that could affect the day (like the fire alarm will be tested at 11am!).

A notice outside the studio saying something along the lines of "Exams in progress. Please be quiet" is always a good idea and cover any windows that people waiting could peer into. The candidates do not need any distractions! It is recommended to cover mirrors in the studio too and this is essential if your students will be facing the mirrors. Check with your examining body for more details.

At break times, continue to look after the examiner as you would look after a guest in your home. Offer hot and cold drinks and something warm for lunch in the winter. Even if facilities are sparse at the venue, you can always bring hot soup in a flask and present it nicely in a bowl on a tray. Always leave the examiner on their own during breaks and make sure your music operator leaves the room too.

Another important way to help your students gain the most on the examining day, especially with younger students, it is so important that they have practiced with the room set out as it will be on exam day. They must also have practiced their entry into the room and their exit. If they are carrying in props or character shoes, etc, do they know what to do with them after they have said good morning or good afternoon to the examiner? Do they know the examiners name so they can greet them with a friendly "good morning Miss X"? Do they know where to stand at the barre, in the centre, for steps across the room? Practice all this, repeatedly, and it well help make the day a really lovely experience for students and examiner. You will also have candidates who will be excited to take their next exam.

Make It Happen!

- Welcome the examiner as you would welcome a special guest to your home
- Make their day as pleasant as possible and you and your students will enjoy it too
- Check out the chair and table for comfort over several hours
- Offer hot and cold drinks and a light lunch
- Leave the examiner on their own in the studio during breaks

Chapter 10

When you reach for
the stars…

I do hope you are now feeling well prepared to start this exciting journey.

You will be making an amazing contribution to the lives of so many people, for many years to come both inside and outside your school.

I hope you feel you are now in a position to start, grow and develop your business and your school. The dance industry is an incredible industry and we are privileged to be a part of it.

Once you have a sound business base for your enterprise, the opportunities are endless. Once you have established the foundations, you can achieve so many other dreams and ambitions and continue to have a positive impact on the lives of so many people.

Keep alive the passion that made you want to teach dance in the first place. Dance teachers have a massive impact on the lives of their students, and often the parents as well. It is an amazing gift to be able to pass on your love for this wonderful art form.

Always remember that not everyone you teach will become another prima ballerina or Fred Astaire. But maybe they will take their own children to watch dance or to join a dance class, thus ensuring there will be jobs for dancers and dance teachers for many more generations to come. What a legacy!

As a dance teacher you will create many poised, disciplined, well-mannered young people who will go through life understanding how to work as a team – because of you.

They will realise that; through hard work and diligent practice anything is possible – because of you.

They will know that dreams really can come true – because of you.

Because this is what dance teachers do. Day in, day out. Let us share our knowledge, our professionalism and our passion with each other, so that, eventually, dance teachers everywhere will be respected as the hugely important professionals within society that they actually are.

And finally: please remember to keep growing your dreams, your goals and your vision as well as keeping alive the passion that you have for this wonderful industry, and you will undoubtedly have a very successful business.

In the iconic lyrics of Anthony Drew from his stage version of *Mary Poppins*:

"If you reach for stars
All you get are the stars
But we've found a whole new spin
If you reach for the Heavens
You get the stars thrown in."

About the author

At the age of eight my mother took me to see the ballet *Sleeping Beauty* at the Royal Court Theatre in Liverpool. It changed my life. "I wanted to **be** the lilac fairy". I was totally spellbound! I immediately asked my mother if I could have ballet lessons and soon decided I wanted to be a ballet teacher.

I was born and brought up in Crosby, Liverpool, where my father was a window cleaner and my mother a schoolteacher. I left school at 16 to go to dance college and very soon was giving dance classes in the local church hall in order to make the money to pay for my own dance training. By the time I was 21, I was renting a dance studio of my own where I taught 150 pupils, ballet, tap and modern dance. I had absolutely no money. I scraped together the rent and that was it.

When the keep fit boom arrived a few years later, I also started offering keep-fit classes for adults. By 1979 I had moved to bigger studios and had two teachers working for me. With the help of a friend, I also started making bright coloured leotards for my pupils to wear in the end-of-term shows I put on at the local theatre.

Most people at that time still wore black or blue nylon leotards and they didn't fit like leotards do now. They were baggy, lumpy garments and I hated seeing my students looking like that, but I realised there was this amazing fabric you could get in bright colours called Lycra. My leotards were soon in demand and a lot of my friends were dance teachers, so they would see them in my shows and ask me to make them some. Initially, I made the leotards on a friend's sewing machine as a favour to other teachers, but as the demand grew, I borrowed £50 from my mother and bought an old industrial sewing machine, which I installed in a friend's attic.

The school was expanding, so I made them at all sorts of bizarre times, sometimes during the day and sometimes late in the evening after class. Harlequin Dancewear (now International Dance Supplies or IDS) was born!

In 1980 I married a Devon man, but continued to run my dance school and make leotards in Crosby during the week and commuted to Devon at the weekend. By 1985 I decided it was time to move to Devon permanently, so I handed over the dance school to a friend and took my sewing machine with me!

By now the dancewear business was a separate entity I was selling to dance teachers and retailers all over the country. In Devon I hired a small unit on an industrial site for £35 a week. To begin with I was on my own – I would sew the leotards myself and then phone round to get orders. Sometimes I would close the place to go and deliver them. In the first year I had sales of £15,000. I took on a couple of machinists and a youth training scheme trainee and when my husband retired, he joined the business too.

Over the years we grew IDS to be one of the biggest local employers distributing our dancewear and costumes around the world. It is wonderful for me to see it continuing to grow and thrive and it has just celebrated its 42nd birthday!

During all these years I stayed in touch with dance teachers as I was the RAD (Royal Academy of Dance) local organiser for the North-West and then the South-West where I was also Chair of the Region at one time. I was instrumental in founding both the North-West and South-West IDTA (International Dance Teachers Association) Areas and was the first Chairman of the North-West Area. I became a trustee of the RAD and was a member of their finance committee for many years and I am currently a trustee of bbodance (British Ballet Organisation). I am a Life Member of RAD

(Royal Academy of Dance), ISTD (Imperial Society of Teachers of Dance) and UKA (United Kingdom Alliance), as well as an Honorary Member of bbodance.

Many of the achievements at IDS were driven by the hopes and dreams I had as a dance teacher and one of my passions is to share the business knowledge I have gained, over so many years, with dance teachers and other business owners.

In 2010 I was delighted to be honoured with an MBE for Services to Business in the Queen's Birthday Honours and I have also been awarded a First Women Award, Everywoman Award and a Stevie Entrepreneur Award. I am proud to be a Patron of Devon Rape Crisis & Sexual Abuse Services as well as Tap Attack, UK Dance Class Championships and Dancing With a Difference.

Lightning Source UK Ltd.
Milton Keynes UK
UKHW011528011219
354565UK00007B/164/P